ANGST

A COLLECTION OF POEMS

BIANCA K. GRAY

To my teenage self who thought there wasn't anything in life worth living for.

CONTENTS

Introduction — vii

1. Numb — 1
2. Sunshine Rays — 4
3. Would you have loved me if I were in color? — 6
4. Parasitic Alien — 8
5. Dreams — 11
6. A messed up girl with nowhere to be — 14
7. Regrets — 15
8. Obsession — 16
9. Heart on my sleeve — 17
10. Pretend — 18
11. Traces of him — 20
12. Moments stolen — 21
13. I'm not real — 23
14. When I was sixteen — 25
15. Unrequited — 27
16. This isn't love — 29
17. She's life's disdain — 31
18. Pep Talk — 32
19. When the moon meets the sun — 33
20. Finally — 34
21. Falling in love — 36
22. Confession — 37
23. Frivolous — 39
24. I never expected someone like you — 41
25. Home — 43

26. Arguments in a relationship 45
27. Quan 46
28. Remember 47
29. Love 50

Acknowledgments 53
Also by Bianca K. Gray 55

INTRODUCTION

This book of poetry is a collection of poems that I wrote when I was, mostly, in my teen years. Some of it is from when I was in high school, and some of it is from when I entered my first ever relationship (and last) in college.

I think everyone can remember how they felt when they were a teenager. How every emotion seemed to wrack your body with every world-shattering event that happened in your life. For me, I felt so much and I felt my emotions so hard. My life started and ended with a simple emotion of happiness or utter despair.

In high school, I was obsessed with romance. I wanted someone who loved me *so much*, that looked at me like I was the sun that rose into the sky every morning. I had so much love to give, so much of myself that I wanted to take apart for someone.

All I thought of love at the time was that it must be something heartbreaking. Something that consumed one's thoughts every waking moment because that's how I felt when I had a crush on someone. It was heartbreaking. It was miserable. It was exhilarating. But, I was never truly in love with anyone. I just wanted to be so much so that I convinced myself that I was.

I recognized in my poetry, throughout the years, that I come to grips with what love really is like as I entered my first relationship. There is a story that goes throughout these poems. Almost a feeling of acceptance, but not quite. But, the recognition of what love is supposed to be, through the eyes of someone navigating their first relationship.

Being a teenager, and having these intense emotions, is a beautiful experience. And, personally, I look back on those moments with fondness, if not a touch of sadness for how I saw myself. But, for anyone who might resonate with these poems, know that it does get better, eventually.

1 / NUMB

Numb.
>That's how I feel most of the time.
>Numb.

Like when it's desperately cold in the wintertime.
>That kind of numb.

Where you don't even feel the pinpricks of pain
>And the skin on your body becomes translucent
>And you can see the blue lines that are your veins.
>Where nothing is good yet nothing is ruined.
>That kind of numb.

But see, that's where things get confusing.

The emptiness succumbs
That kind of numb slowly undoing.

And all I can see is a bright light
    A bright light that has your eyes
    In a place where all I could see was the black of night
    And now suddenly all I feel are manufactured highs.

What am I trying to say?
    See, what used to bring me back was pain.
    But now, what brings me back is a cliché.
    You make me feel something, which is insane.

I can't get the taste of you off of my tongue
    The phantom of your touches on my skin
    The sound of your name constricting my lungs
    Just having all five senses feels somewhat like a sin.

You've shown me what it's like to feel
    I finally feel somewhat real.
    Yet, it always comes back, that feeling of numb.
    A sickness, a demon that even love can't overcome.
    I feel that kind of numb.

- BECAUSE FEELINGS ARE TEMPORARY WHILE NOTHING STRETCHES OUT

FOREVER

2 / SUNSHINE RAYS

There's a girl who's black and white with shades of gray,
But there's a boy who loves the rainbow in sunshine rays.

There's a girl who's not a brilliant rose but a wildflower
But there's a boy who notices her during the golden hour.

When the sun starts to set and everything is aglow,
When the shadows creep towards him and start to grow,

That's when the boy notices the girl for a while,
And that's when he can see her godforsaken smile.

The girl may be black and white with shades of gray,
But to him, she's as colorful as a rainbow in sunshine rays.

- PERHAPS HE CAN SEE ME

3 / WOULD YOU HAVE LOVED ME IF I WERE IN COLOR?

You once told me that you liked sunsets.
    You liked how the sky would burst into color before turning into darkness.

I was a night sky and I thought that the moon and stars would be enough,
    But a night sky has no color to dream of.

I'm sorry that all I can offer is a useless moon
    And a handful of stars.

I wish I could set the sky ablaze.
    I wish I could give you fire.

. . .

Even though it's not a sunset, the night sky is yours.
I am sorry that I cannot give you more.

- BUT WOULD YOU HAVE LOVED ME IF I WERE IN COLOR?

4 / PARASITIC ALIEN

Always used to be bright
In my head.

Now it's as dark as night.
Everything is dead.

What happened
Between then and now?

I've been inhabited
By something I don't allow.

It takes no form nor shape,
Slowly going with the air.

There is no escape
Because, about you, it doesn't care.

It gets inside your mind
Digging its claws into your soul.

Its motto is "Gone with the kind,
And in with the miserable cold."

All my flowers have died.
Inside I'm falling apart.

My own happiness tied.
Its darkness, an art.

It gets inside all your crevices,
Turning what is into what was.

It's turning me into ashes,
This thing is the cause.

It won't get out of my head,
Feeding me dark thoughts.

It lives off of my dread,
While happiness *rots*.

- THEY SAY IT GETS BETTER, BUT IT NEVER DOES

5 / DREAMS

I keep dreaming...
    A dreadful dream where I'm falling.

One may call it a nightmare
    Made specifically for me, *my* nightmare.

In it, I'm stuck in a velvet case,
    Dark as night and lined with lace.

I'm screaming, but no one hears
    As I slowly start to drown on tears.

But then, the bottom slowly does open,

I fall, nothing cushions
This horrible fall, where everything breaks.
I cannot move, not even my head can shake.

I realize then, that I am dying.
    Isn't this what you wanted? I'm sighing.

As my eyes are closing, I'm reaching out
    Towards a face, but I have a doubt.

The face is sneering, it is me.
    But how can that be?

I'll tell you how, exactly.
    I am my own enemy.

I'm the one who put me in that case
    Dark as night and lined with lace.
I'm the one who opened the bottom,
    Falling through cold chill air of autumn.

I'm the one who is the murderer,
    My own murderer.

        . . .

I killed me.
    I'll never be free.

- A RECURRING NIGHTMARE THAT NEVER LEFT

6 / A MESSED UP GIRL WITH NOWHERE TO BE

I can't stand watching you look at me
While you wipe my tears and see
A messed up girl with nowhere to be.

But, I also can't stand to watch you leave,
Which always happens, inevitably.

This is why I'm doing this, you see.
Not for you, but I guess for me.

- AN ATTEMPT TO STOP

7 / REGRETS

Your hands felt like fire,
   While mine were cold as ice.

And I thought if I let you touch me,
   I would finally feel alive.

- for a fleeting moment, I thought you'd warm me up

8 / OBSESSION

I leave my window slightly open every day
In hopes that you'll crawl in with the sun's rays.

But thoughts of you do not come in the morning.
Instead,
Thoughts of you are constantly crawling around in my head.

- AND I NEED IT TO STOP

9 / HEART ON MY SLEEVE

They say home is where the heart is, but my heart has never stayed in one place.

I'm a wandering soul without a home, if that's the case.

But even though my wanderlust self belongs nowhere,
I have to say that I see my heart everywhere.

- BE CAREFUL WHEN WEARING YOUR HEART ON YOUR SLEEVE

10 / PRETEND

Hold me, as if you'll never hold again
And don't hesitate or abstain.

Let me breathe you in.
Let me feel at home again.

Even if it's just for pretend,
Let's pretend one more second.

Let me pretend that I'm yours.
Just one second more, let me be yours.

- LIE TO ME

11 / TRACES OF HIM

After a while, I wasn't me anymore.

I was just pieces of him.

Traces of him.

- how long has it been?

12 / MOMENTS STOLEN

All I can remember are fragments,
    Late night whispers
    Hands that touched like magnets
    Words spoken without filters.

All I can remember are your eyes,
    Cavernous brown and almond
    Golden with the sunrise.

All I can remember is wishing,
    Eyelash flutters and lips close to kissing.

All I can remember are lies.
    Touches that burned

And sleep deprived highs.

All I remember are moments.
    But they were moments stolen.

- AND MOMENTS THAT WEREN'T MEANT FOR ME.

13 / I'M NOT REAL

There's a smile playing on my lips
And a swing to my hips.

But there's bags under my eyes
And lips that tell of lies.

Of "I'm fines" and laughter
A joke or two to drive it home after.

But there's something wrong inside
Because something needed has died.

I'm not a zombie, but I'm the living dead.
The whispers are getting louder in my head.

I'm numb. I feel nothing.
Just another body that's breathing.

Notice that I don't feel.
Realize that I'm not real.

- I'm numb I'm numb I'm numb

14 / WHEN I WAS SIXTEEN

When I was sixteen, I fell in love.
    He didn't look like love.
    Not what I'd expect from love.

He looked like a Monday.
    No expectations and dismal.

He felt like a Friday.
    All weekend highs and anticipation.

But, he turned out to be Sunday.
    The end of something great or awful.
    But the end, just the same.

            . . .

When I was sixteen, I fell in love.
    He didn't look like love.
    Or what I expected from love.
    But that's because he just wasn't love.

- THINGS I WISH I COULD TELL MY YOUNGER SELF

15 / UNREQUITED

The skin around my eyes are black and blue
From lack of sleep and thoughts of you.

The nights are filled with wishful thinking
And aching chests, hearts sinking.

Unrequited visions dance around in my sight
The sound of hearts breaking fills the silence of the night.

And I'm left here laying with my thoughts
So here's to dark circles and broken hearts.

- A TOAST TO UNREQUITED LOVE

16 / THIS ISN'T LOVE

When he's around, everything hurts.
    This isn't love, but I think it's close.
    No, this isn't love, it's worse.

When he's near, I can't breathe.
    It's like lungs collapsing
    But, with no hope of relief.

He's everything I want to be
    And everything I think I need.

But being near him hurts.
    Looking at him hurts.
    So, this can't be love, it's just worse.

- AND I CAN'T TAKE IT ANYMORE

17 / SHE'S LIFE'S DISDAIN

Born to suffering, born to pain,
    The world's too much for her
    The world's too vain.

Her voice unheard,
    Her life mundane.
    When does it all end?
    She's life's disdain.

- TOO MUCH ALL AT ONCE

18 / PEP TALK

What I want to do and where I want to go isn't determined by intelligence.
I know decisions are important, but listen for just a second.

Life is there for you to actually *live*.
Why are our brains and hearts combative?

Do what you want and want what you do.
Why are you letting fear get to you?

- REMINDERS

19 / WHEN THE MOON MEETS THE SUN

You are day while I am night
   You're full of blue skies and sunshine, while I only have starlight.

And just like the sun, your beauty is blinding
   Warmth radiates when you're only smiling.

And when the moon meets the sun, it gets a little brighter.
   And just like that, when I met you, I got a little lighter.

- YOU'RE THE PERSONIFICATION OF SUNSHINE

20 / FINALLY

I'm breathing you in
As you pull me in closer.
The sweet smell of your skin
Is everywhere and all over.

This feeling is a lot like drinking,
Intoxicating and dizzy.
And all I'm thinking
Is that you're making me tipsy.

You set me on fire.
Just a single touch of yours
Puts me on the brink of desire
And all I want is more.

> In your hands, let me combust.
> Set me on fire 'til I'm only ash and dust.

- CLOSE JUST ISN'T CLOSE ENOUGH

21 / FALLING IN LOVE

Please don't ever let go
    The thought of you leaving aches me so.

I never thought I could love someone this much
    Or that I would ever let my soul be touched.

But, here I am, open and vulnerable.
    So being hurt by you would simply be unbearable.

Please take care of my heart.
    Because it'll forever be yours, even if you depart.

- I'm terrified

22 / CONFESSION

All I know is that your smile is pure sunshine
And you make even the living dead feel alive.

That when you're around
The desperately loud world doesn't make a sound.

You make the voices in my head go quiet.
You make me feel comfortable in silence.

To you, I'm nothing more or nothing less.
I'm just me.
And that's all I ever wanted anyone to see.

I can't put how I feel about you in words.
But these letters together comes pretty close:

I love you.
But that, you already knew.

- LOVE LOVE LOVE IS SO HARD TO EXPLAIN

23 / FRIVOLOUS

My hands shake as if I'm in withdrawal and suddenly got my fix when you're near.

My breath catches in my throat, my lungs burn from lack of oxygen because who needs oxygen when you're here?

It's frivolous and ridiculous, I know...

But I'm afraid, terrified actually, that if I speak, you'll go.

Because the people that I have cared about the most

Have always left me because of my words, have turned into ghosts.

. . .

Because the people that I hold close,
    I always seem to reproach.

- ABANDONMENT ISSUES?

24 / I NEVER EXPECTED SOMEONE LIKE YOU

I never expected someone like you.

You are everything I've ever dreamed of.
    You are more than enough.

You are the first rays of sunlight that warm my face.
    You, just as you are, are my safest place.

You're the most gentle man I've ever known.
    And you scare me because you represent the unknown.

I never knew love could feel like this.

All I knew was that love was the furthest thing from bliss.

But, you've changed that... and me.
    You are love, and you've found me finally.

I never expected you, you see.
    I never expected love to set me free.

- I ALWAYS THOUGHT LOVE WAS A TRAP, BUT YOU SHOWED ME OTHERWISE

25 / HOME

Dark and cold of a long night
Tossing and turning back and forth
Only finding comfort from a phone's light
Looking for the star pointed north.

They say you gotta find your way home
But my home isn't a place.
My mind keeps wandering, it roams.
It's consumed by a face.

It means my home is shaky.
It's not guaranteed.
Because that face is associated with safety,
But, can a human be believed?

Words are words are words
Until they're not anymore.
They say love lasts but I've seen that it erodes.
So what exactly are we falling for?

Dark and cold of a long night
Tossing and turning side to side
Constantly thinking of this love plight
But love is a decision that I get to decide.

My home is shaky and it's not guaranteed.
But I'd choose you a hundred times over so with love,
I'll proceed.

- I'LL ALWAYS CHOOSE YOU

26 / ARGUMENTS IN A RELATIONSHIP

The air is getting thicker

My lungs are getting weaker

And my hands and lips are eager

After every moment we bicker.

- anxiety

27 / QUAN

Made of stardust
   And a dash of sunshine

He's love promised
   And hope combined.

       - because he's night and day and all the details in between

28 / REMEMBER

Remember me.
Remember when we laughed over our first kiss
How clumsy we were and how I missed
And how my nerves were shot to bits
And even though we were new at this
That we were in complete and utter bliss.

Remember me.
Remember the night you ducked your head
On that bench where you immediately regretted what you said
Words that slightly filled you with dread
And words that normally made me fled
But lighted a fire inside of me instead.

Remember me.
Remember that night where we set each other on fire
Where you taught me what it was like to desire
And given each other a feeling that was never felt prior
Where under a golden glow, we admired
And felt the other's full gaze in its entire.

Remember me.
Remember how fragile our egos were
And how we were incredibly insecure
Over situations that were entirely pure
And how we reminded that we were "yours"
So quickly were we over it and just as sure.

Remember me.
Remember those nights where we fought
How our words wrecked us with fraught
And how our stomachs were tied up with knots
But how those bitter words were for naught
And how we still, for each other, were besot.

Remember us.
Remember how we love like no other
How we made each other better

How you were such a charmer
And how your words made my face change color
And that we always promise forever.

Remember that you love me
Remember how that love sets us free.

And remember that I'll always love you
And all that you do.

- TO YOU, FOR YOU

29 / LOVE

"Love" is not the right word to say.

It does not contain the emotion that I feel.

When you stand in front of me, it's like you're not real.

You see, when you're not there, the day is gray.

And when you're not there, it's like I forgot how to feel.

You make me feel something that I've concealed.

For when you smiled and then did look my way,

I knew then that I would never be the same.

For when I looked into your starlit eyes

My heart began to race and I knew whom to blame.

And I knew that if you were to be my demise,

I'd be all right with that. For your name

Would be the last to leave my lips.
Your hands, the last that touch my hips.

— A SONNET

ACKNOWLEDGMENTS

Thank you to my loving fiancé who taught me what it was like to love myself, truly. You showed me what love was supposed to be like, what it was supposed to feel like. You showed me endless support in who I was, and loved me despite the weirdness of who I am. I was never too weird for you, never too annoying. And for that, I will always appreciate you until the day that I take my last breath. You are truly the last name that I will ever speak and I will love you until the day that I die.

Thank you to my cover artist, Laurel Mosher!! You have been through all my emotions from high school, and you were there for me through it all. I appreciate your friendship and thank you for blessing me with your TALENT!! Your covers are always to die for and you have supported me the MOST through my writing ventures. You're the bestest friend one could ever have.

Thank you to those of you who suffered through my emotions in high school. I was known for liking a new boy every week, and for those boys, I'm deeply sorry, haha. I probably freaked you out with how intense I was. It wasn't really YOU that made me feel that way, it was romantic comedies honestly. And that mickey mouse company. Darn that mickey mouse company and their princess movies.

And thank you to my lovely parents who raised me during this tumultuous time in my life. You did your best with me and I appreciate you two so very much!!

ALSO BY BIANCA K. GRAY

The Celestials

- A fantasy story that takes place in a parallel universe called Asynithis. Magical creatures rule and Khalon needs to save the world from utter destruction. Will he be able to protect the Gods that he once hated? Or will he let Asynithis fall into oblivion?

Fine

- Grace Lee has never liked Jayden King. Ever. But, when she finds herself dead, and as a ghost, she needs Jayden's help to find out who her real murderer is. In the process, she gets to know him better and maybe realizes that... Jayden is actually... a nice guy?

Made in the USA
Columbia, SC
01 June 2022